PLAYGROUND EDUCATION

CREATED and WRITTEN by

R. TOBIAS PITTMAN

THE EDUCATIONAL PANDA

PUGSLEY PANDA

ILLUSTRATIONS by

William Chislum

EDITED by

Gloria Miles

Playground Education and Entertainment
www.pugsleypanda.com | email: pugsleypanda@gmail.com

Hello Safety Sam, where are you and Pugsley going?
Hello Kayla, Pugsley and I are on our way to give safety tips to children. Let's go!
Wellington Hill St

Fall also means Halloween. Do you have any safety tips for Trick or Treaters?
Sure Kayla and Pugsley, follow me.
Blake Street

December means winter, do you have any winter safety tips?
I sure do, come on Kayla.
Morton Street

Ormond Street
HELP...
Never bury anyone in the snow, as there may be a risk of suffocation.
That could be dangerous.

We sure learned a lot about safety.
That's why you are one of the Educational Kidz.
That's me, Safety Sam.
Ashmont Sta

Educational Kid

SAFETY SAM

ENJOY ALL THESE OTHER CHILDREN'S BOOKS FROM

PLAYGROUND EDUCATION

"No Bullying"
By
Safety Sam

"Wellington Hill Playground"
By
The Educational Kidz

"Famous Landmarks in The United States"
By
Geography Gerald

"Seasonal Safety Tips for Children"
By
Safety Sam

"How Does Water Recycle "
By
Science Scott

PUGSLEY PANDA

www.ingramcontent.com/pod-product-compliance
Lightning Source LLC
LaVergne TN
LVHW072109070426
835509LV00002B/88